LifeCaps Presents:

Pelé

A Biography of Edson Arantes do Nascimento

By Frank Foster

BookCaps™ Study Guides
www.bookcaps.com

Table of Contents

About LifeCaps

LifeCaps is an imprint of BookCaps™ Study Guides. With each book, a lesser known or sometimes forgotten life is is recapped. We publish a wide array of topics (from baseball and music to literature and philosophy), so check our growing catalogue regularly (**www.bookcaps.com**) to see our newest books.

Introduction

Pelé! Pelé! Pelé! It was a familiar chant, a chant which had been screamed from the terraces for nearly thirty years. It was October 1977, and the final game of Pelé's hugely successful career had just finished. As Pelé looked around the stadium, tears were streaming down his face, his emotions running wild. But what an amazing journey it had been. It was all a far cry from the scene that Pelé was born into, some thirty-seven years earlier.

Chapter 1: Childhood

Edson Arantes do Nascimento was born in the Brazilian city of Três Corações, just north of Rio de Janeiro, on 23rd October 1940, despite the incorrect date of his birth certificate of 21st October. Pelé, as well all know him by, was not born into riches or stardom. Pelé's mother, Dona Celeste, the daughter of a cart driver, gave birth to Pelé in a small, unappealing house built of second-hand bricks. Pelé's family were not desperately poor, but they had little money. Life was certainly not easy.

Pelé's father, Joao Ramos do Nascimento (or Dondinho), played football at amateur level for Atletico of Tres Coracoes. He was generally regarded of as a good player, and had particular prowess with his head, once scoring five goals in one match with it.

Maybe Dondiho had a premonition. Upon his first sight of his new baby boy, he prodded his legs and apparently remarked, "This one will be a great footballer!" How right he was![1]

---

[1] Pelé, *Pelé the Autobiography*, (Kingsway, London: Simon & Schuster, 2006), pp. 13-14.

Pelé's real first name, Edson, was a tribute to Thomas Edison, the inventor of the light bulb. The arrival of electricity in the Nascimento household just before Pelé's birth was quite an event, and so it felt only natural to pay some kind of tribute to Edison.

The nickname of 'Pelé' came some years later. Pelé actually wanted to be a goalkeeper when he was very young, and his hero was a goalkeeper for Vasco de São Lourenço whose nickname was Bilé. A young Edson could not pronounce his nickname properly, and use to mistakenly call him Pelé. Pelé's friends and relatives then started to mock Edson by calling him Pelé. This infuriated Pelé, but eventually, the nickname stuck. What an iconic name it has turned out to be.

Just before Pelé's fourth birthday, in September of 1944, the Nascimento family moved to Bauru. Pelé's father had been offered a new job as a local government functionary, and also received an offer to play football for a club there. This move would change young Pelé's life. Bauru was something completely alien for young Pelé, his brother Zoca and his sister Maria Lucia. A city of 800,000 people at the time, it felt like the centre of the world to their young wide eyes. It was a new beginning for the family.

The government functionary job didn't materialise for Dondinho. To make matters worse, Dondinho's knee problems, which he had suffered with for years, began to flare up, preventing him from playing football. Times were hard for Dondinho and his family, and they struggled financially for some time. Pelé and his siblings were always barefoot, with few clothes, and at times they ate as little as some bread and a slice of banana.

Pelé would take it on himself as the eldest of the siblings to do his bit to help his family stay afloat. He went out offering his services of shoe-shining to the more affluent people of his neighbourhood. He practiced on a pair of shoes his aunt gave him, but, having played football barefoot all his life, one day he tried out playing with his shoes. Needless to say, he eventually ruined them. The shoe-shining eventually progressed to the football stadium of Bauru Athletic Club and at the railway stations. His father managed to find some work at a health clinic and the Pelé household began to receive a much-needed steady income.

Pelé began school at Ernesto Monte primary school. Pelé wasn't a great student, but not a highly disruptive one either. A young Pelé actually dreamed of being a pilot, and even skipped school to head down to the airfield, marvelling at the planes before him. This dream, however, was short-lived. Pelé and his friends witnessed the autopsy of a dead pilot through a hospital window. He had been killed in a plane accident. This horrified Pelé and from then on, he didn't visit the airfield again.

Pelé was a restless child, acting on impulse, and he was quite a handful for his teachers at his school. Pelé's time at school involved misbehaviour, chattering and mischief. Physical punishment from his teachers was commonplace. This did not really stop the cheeky young Pelé from his mischievous acts, though! One day he even climbed up a mango tree in the yard next to the school and threw down mangoes for all of his friends![2]

[2] Pelé, *Pelé the Autobiography*, (Kingsway, London: Simon & Schuster, 2006), p.27.

An impressionable Pelé saw his father's footballing ability and naturally wanted to emulate him. Football was in Pelé's genes. Pelé was surrounded by football in his childhood. He would dream about football and when he could next play. He, along with his friends, played with a sock stuffed with paper, which had been shaped into a ball and tied with a piece of string. There were other improvisations Pelé and his gang came up with as well to mimic a football. They played in the nearby streets of his neighbourhood, and it was on these streets that Pelé began honing his legendary skills. Football began to become an obsession for Pelé. All thoughts of any other profession evaporated from his mind. Pelé wanted to be a footballer.

An entrepreneurial Pelé decided that a club must be made, which the players living on the neighbouring streets of Sete de Setembro and Rubens Arruda would represent. Soon Pelé and his friends started to conjure up ideas of how to get enough money to buy a ball, kits and boots. The youngsters eventually devised a plan to steal peanuts from train wagons, and then sell them at the doors of the circus and the cinema! This venture gave them enough money to buy vests and shorts, but no socks, boots or t-shirts. Still, they were now a team with some semblance of a kit, and they began to compete with teams from other neighbourhoods.

Pelé's original plan to get what they needed was to sell or trade a completed football sticker album. They managed to complete their sticker album, and Pelé exchanged it for a proper football. The team usually played on Pelé's road and soon they became known in the area. Not many teams wanted to play them, and they were apparently unbeaten.

Pelé's father began to take more of an active interest in Pelé's football after witnessing his young son's obvious natural talent. He began coaching him a little, focusing on developing Pelé's touch, his left foot and his heading ability. Moves synonymous with Pelé's game such as the shoulder feint, the short strides in possession and the changing of pace whilst dribbling were all taught to Pelé by his father during those years.

Pelé's mother, on the other hand, was not too impressed. She was worried about the lack of time Pelé spent studying. She thought football was a waste of time, and actually wanted Pelé to become a doctor. Her only experience of football was through her husband, and this did not bear much fruit for the family. To her, football was something detracting from real work and didn't guarantee food on the table. She would bellow at her husband to stop playing with his son, and Dondinho would shout back, "The boy can't kick with his left foot and I'm just teaching him – that's all!"[3]

Pelé remembers the 1950 World Cup final between Brazil and Uruguay vividly to this day. Coming into the final, Brazil, as hosts and favourites, were expected to come out victorious, which would have given Brazil their first World Cup triumph. Dondinho had arranged a party on the day of the match to celebrate. Without television, the coverage was brought to them all through the radio, and everybody gathered round to listen to the match unfolding.

---

[3] Pelé, *Pelé the Autobiography*, (Kingsway, London: Simon & Schuster, 2006), pp.40-1.

Pelé and his friends had been dividing their time during the match between playing football outside, and running in to listen to the latest developments. He ran in after the final whistle and was greeted with stunned silence. Uruguay had stunned the whole of Brazil with a 2-1 victory.

Everybody was shocked. This was the first time Pelé had seen grown men showing such emotion. There were tears all round, including from Dondinho.

Upon seeing all this, Pelé tried to comfort his father and promised him, "One day, I'll win you the World Cup". Little did everybody know that these were words of gold.

Pelé ran to his father's room where he spoke to a picture of Jesus on the wall, crying and asking why Brazil had lost. He wailed: "You know if I had been there I wouldn't have let Brazil lose".[4] Eight years later Pelé did not let Brazil lose.

It was around this time that Pelé began playing for a few different clubs in and around Bauru. He played on Saturdays and Sundays for a few different teams. His love of the game was only growing, and he would play for hours on end.

[4] Pelé, *Pelé the Autobiography*, (Kingsway, London: Simon & Schuster, 2006), pp.45-8.

Pelé was also still playing for his street side that were now known as Ameriquinha. The team's original name was 'The Shoeless Ones!' The team had started to train more seriously, practicing persistently. The hard work was paying off, and the skills of the youngsters were improving by the day. In a tournament which the mayor of Bauru had organised for small neighbourhood clubs, Ameriquinha got to the final, despite playing against players several years older than they were.

The final was held in the stadium in which Dondinho played, with thousands of spectators looking on. Ameriquinha won the final, and Pelé came out as top goal scorer. And, for the first time in his life, Pelé heard what would soon become a very familiar chant in any stadium Pelé graced: "Pelé, Pelé, Pelé!"

In 1954, Pelé was invited to join Baquinho or "Little BAC", a junior club of the club Dondinho played for, Bauru Athletic Club. The coach of the team was Waldemar de Brito, a man who was one of Brazil's best players of the 1930s and '40s. After signing for Baquinho, Pelé penned his first contract at 13 years of age.

Waldemar de Brito was a man who believed in the virtues of discipline and hard work, and these virtues soon rubbed off on Pelé. He taught Pelé and his teammates lots of new techniques, how to read the game, how to move off the ball and how to receive the ball. He was teaching Pelé the aspects of the game which make a player not just good, but great.

After a couple of years, Baquinho's team began to break up after Waldemar de Brito resigned as coach. Players were leaving and times were changing. Pelé, too, was looking to move on. A potential move to play for Bangu in Rio de Janeiro fell through after Pelé's mother refused to accept it. Waldemar de Brito was the one to engineer Pelé's next career move.

Waldemar visited Pelé's parents and told them he had been in discussions with the president of Santos. Waldemar was a real admirer of Pelé's talents, and he made it clear to Pelé's parents that there was an opportunity for Pelé to join Santos. Santos were state champions and had a good team. Waldemar believed that Pelé could progress through the ranks quickly at Santos.

His persistence eventually paid off, and Pelé's mother grudgingly agreed to the move, on the condition that Waldemar would go with her young boy. Waldemar agreed. Pelé was about to embark on the move of a lifetime, and begin a love affair with the club forever.[5]

[5] Pelé, *Pelé the Autobiography*, (Kingsway, London: Simon & Schuster, 2006), pp.57-8.

Chapter 2: Early Playing Days

The move to São Paolo was going to be an adventure of a lifetime for the fifteen year-old Pelé. He had some fears, but he also realised what an opportunity he had. It was a chance to discover life. Very early one Sunday morning, Pelé made his way to the train station, ready to embark on the first journey of his trip to Santos. The farewell to his grandmother Ambrosina, Uncle Jorge, siblings and parents was an emotional one. At the train station, his mother and sister Zoca could not hold back their tears. As Pelé waved them off, he struggled to hold back his own too.

At the train station in São Paolo, Pelé and his father met Waldemar. After some lunch they headed to Santos. Waldemar gave Pelé some golden advice on the journey, he told him not to be awed by the players around him and to play as if he was having a kick about in Bauru. He told him to never listen to the radio or to read the newspapers. His final piece of advice was influenced by Waldemar's promise to Pelé's beloved mother, "no smoking, no drinking, no women and no hanging around with a bad crowd".[6]

That same Sunday, Waldemar took Pelé and his father to a match between Santos and Comercial. After the match, Pelé was introduced to the Santos coach Luis Alonso. Players such as Jair, Zito and Pepe were all introduced to Pelé also, and he was awestruck. The Santos players made Pelé feel comfortable and said to Pelé's father, "We'll take care of the boy!" Soon after Pelé said his final goodbyes to Waldemar and his father, and with that, Pelé was officially a footballer of Santos.

[6] Pelé, *Pelé the Autobiography*, (Kingsway, London: Simon & Schuster, 2006), pp.62-3.

Pelé assumed he would be training with players of his own tender age, but to his surprise, he was immediately thrown in with the professionals for his first training session. Pelé was extremely nervous. He was very slight, at less than 60 kilos, and when the rain began to come down, his legs were shaking in the oversized kit he was wearing. Yet, on the pitch, Pelé was utterly fearless. His marker was the Brazil international Formiga, but Pelé managed to dribble past him twice, impressing the coach and his teammates immediately. Pelé would not play competitively with the first team though, and played with the U 18's and U 20's as his game and physique developed. He was told by Luis Alonso to work on developing his body, and Pelé would also spend hours by himself practicing and perfecting his technique and skills.

Pelé was soon offered a preliminary contract with Santos. Pelé made his way back to his hometown Bauru to see if his parents would agree to the terms of the contract. Pelé's mother and grandmother were distraught to realise that Pelé could potentially be moving to Santos for good. They thought his time at Santos was simply a trial. Their sadness soon began to affect Pelé, and not being able to bear his family being in such sadness, he decided that he could not return to Santos.

Again, Waldemar stepped in to calm the anxieties and sadness of Pelé's family. He convinced everybody including Pelé that the deal was a good one and things would run smoothly. Pelé soon made his way back to Santos to sign the contract.

Pelé carried on training with the first team and playing with the junior teams, being used as an attacking midfielder. Originally, Pelé was playing as an 'armador' or supporting midfielder. The exceptional Del Vecchio and Vasconcelos played in Pelé's position in the first team, and the youngster knew it would be difficult to get a chance in the first team. A perfect opportunity arose for Pelé when a practice game was arranged for the first team in which some first team players would not be playing. Pelé took his chance scoring four goals in a 6-1 victory for Santos. It was beginning to become clear just how much potential this young boy from Baurua had. The press were soon calling for Pelé to be given a proper run in the first team.

Pelé was becoming comfortable with his new life in the beach city of Santos surrounded by his footballing family, and on 7th September 1956, Pelé finally got his chance to play for the Santos first team in a proper match, which was a friendly. Pelé came on in the second half for Del Vecchio, and within minutes he had scored his first official goal of the 1,281 he would go on to score in his career. At just fifteen years of age, Pelé had scored for Santos in his very first match.

The excitement for this talented youngster began to spread locally. At Santos, he was very well known amongst the supporters. In reserve matches in which he played there were crowds of up to 10,000 spectators.

Pelé's friend, Vasconcelos, picked up a horrendous injury in a hugely important match between São Paolo and Santos, where he broke his leg. Vasconcelos was never the same player after this injury, and eventually moved on. Pelé knew that his chance for regular football in the first team would soon come.

Pelé's official debut for Santos came on 12th January 1957 when the Brazilian side came up against Swedish outfit AIK in a tournament. This was Pelé's first big test, and he played well. From that point on, Pelé and Del Vecchio were rotated and both played regularly.

At sixteen years of age, Pelé was now eligible to sign a professional contract with Santos. On the 8th April 1957 he signed an eighteen month deal. Pelé was playing regularly and consistently for Santos, scoring a number of goals, but was still not really garnering nationwide attention. This soon changed during a tournament which was comprised of four Brazilian teams and four European teams. One of the Brazilian teams was made up of Santos and Vasco de Gama players. Pelé was picked to play as centre-forward.

The first match was between the Santos/Vasco team and Beleneses of Portugal. The game was to be played at the world-famous Maracana stadium, the same stadium in which Brazil's tragedy against Uruguay back in 1950 took place. The stadium was packed to the rafters, and Pelé played magnificently, scoring a hat trick. In the two other encounters against Flamengo and São Paolo, Pelé also made the score sheet. Pelé had really impressed, and the national team was soon knocking.

Chapter 3: Early Career and 1958 World Cup

Pelé's debut for the national team came against Argentina in the Copa Roca in July of 1957. The Copa Roca was a traditional match between the two South American giants over two legs. In the first leg, Brazil lost 2-1, with Pelé on the scoresheet. In the return leg Brazil won 2-0, with Pelé opening the scoring. The Copa Roca was just the first of many international titles Pelé would go on to win.

Pelé picked up a knee injury just before the start of the World Cup of 1958 in Sweden. Pelé's World Cup hopes were in the balance, and it was a real possibility that he would not make the final squad. Pelé was fraught with nerves. He was eventually picked and along with the rest of the Brazilian squad, he got on the plane to Europe. The Brazil squad stayed in Italy for a little while, playing two friendlies against Fiorentina and Internazionale. Pelé did not play a part in either game. The squad arrived in Sweden for the World Cup six days prior to their first game. Their group comprised themselves, Austria, England and USSR.

The squad resided in a comfortable hotel, and quickly the squad really began to bond. They had nicknames for one another and would often play jokes on each other too. It was a healthy, spirited atmosphere in the camp and they had an inclination that they may do well. Brazil was a team littered with top quality players and their preparation had been excellent.

In Brazil's first two matches, they beat Austria 3-0 and drew against England 0-0. Pelé didn't play a part in either game, his knee still causing him trouble. For the third game against the USSR, Pelé was ready. He had trained well beforehand, and the time had come for Pelé's first match at a World Cup. There was a lot of interest surrounding the game. The USSR had some fantastic players including legendary goalkeeper Lev Yashin. The press started to take notice when an unknown seventeen year-old was named in the starting line-up. This was the moment Pelé had wished for his whole life; the chance to represent Brazil at a World Cup. He was filled with an enormous sense of pride before kick-off, but knew he had to remain focused on the task in hand.

Brazil played magnificently from the first whistle, and hit the post twice in the first few minutes before taking the lead through midfielder, Vava. Vava scored again in the second half to seal the victory for Brazil and take them to the quarter-finals. Pelé had played fairly well in the match and hit the woodwork in those first few minutes. He was playing with a little anxiety though, and his knee was certainly not 100%. He replayed the match in his head once the team got back to the hotel, and was not very happy with his performance.

In the quarter-finals, Brazil met Wales. This was the Wales team of the great John Charles, but luckily for Brazil, the imposing Welshman was injured for the match. It was a tight affair at 0-0, until Pelé came up trumps. The elegant Didi laid on a pass to Pelé, which he received with his back to the goal. He chested the ball down, turned, beat a man, and then finished with aplomb, tucking the ball into the bottom corner to win the match. It was to be the first goal of many in the World Cup for Pelé. The whole world now began to take note. The confidence this goal gave Pelé was immeasurable.

In the semi-final, Brazil met France. France was a talented side which included striker Just Fontaine, who finished the competition with thirteen goals – a World Cup record. At half-time, the score was 2-1 with two goals from Didi and one from Fontaine. In the second-half, Pelé stole the show, scoring a hat-trick, an unbelievable feat for a seventeen year-old playing in a World Cup semi-final. France could not cope with his pace and dribbling, Pelé almost tormenting them at times. If people in the footballing world hadn't heard of Pelé, they had now. This young boy was setting the world alight. The match finished 5-2, and Brazil was in the World Cup final.

On the 29th June 1958, Brazil met Sweden in the World Cup final. Pelé had accomplished his dream of playing in the World Cup final, but there was still another dream to be realised: to win the competition. Pelé had a vision of his father, Dondinho, crouched over the radio back in Bauru listening in on an immensely proud day for the Nascimento family. The spectators, mainly consisting of supporters of the hosts, erupted in celebration after Sweden opened the scoring within four minutes. Brazil remained calm, and by half-time they were 2-1 up after legendary winger Garrincha twice set up Vava to score. In a similar fashion to the semi-final, the second half belonged to Brazil. Pelé made it 3-1 with a goal of supreme quality. Pelé controlled a long ball on his chest and chipped it over a defender's head. He then ran around the side of the defender, before meeting the ball on the volley and striking it home. It was a marvellous goal, the type of which was rarely seen in those days. To do this on the biggest stage of them all, at seventeen years of age, really showed just how special this young, skinny boy was.

Brazil made it 4-1 through Mario Zagallo before Sweden scored a second. Pelé then wrapped up the match for Brazil when he outjumped two defenders, and executed a looping header into the corner of the net. Brazil were world champions for the first time. Pelé had made good on his promise eight years ago to win the World Cup for Brazil. The heartache of the 1950 World Cup was no longer so bad. Brazil had won the World Cup, thanks in large part to a relatively unknown seventeen year-old. Pelé was overcome with emotion at the end of the match, as were all his teammates. They cried in relief and joy as the realisation they were world champions sank in. One thing was for sure though; Pelé was desperate to taste this sweet success again. This was just the beginning.

Soon after the World Cup, Pelé was now world famous. He appeared on the front of magazines and newspapers worldwide. When they returned home, Brazil were greeted with a raucous reception as they disembarked from the plane, but when they arrived in Rio, the celebrations were on a wholly different scale, with hordes of fans lining the streets in every direction they looked.

An arrangement was made for the Brazil team meet their parents in the offices of a TV network. Pelé met his relatives there, and all their emotions took over as they cried in joy. Here was little Edson as a world champion.

The following days were filled with celebrations and parties throughout Brazil. The team were treated to meals, congratulations, parties and met a whole host of important people. It was all a bit of a blur for Pelé, but one thing was for sure: Pelé's life would certainly never be the same. Particularly in his home town of Bauru, Pelé was a hero. Pelé was also rewarded with a new contract by Santos, and he was able to buy his family's house in Bauru outright, meaning that the family would no longer need to pay any rent.

Chapter 4: Santos Domination

Pelé's iconic number ten shirt became his own during his first full season with Santos. Del Vecchio had left the club and Pelé had established himself as a permanent fixture in the Santos side. His training regime and eating habits changed, and Pelé bulked up dramatically, putting on a lot of muscle. Pelé trained relentlessly which included spending hours working on his weaker left foot and heading. Pelé also took up Karate and Judo, which helped give him the exceptional balance and agility which he was famous for.

Back in those days, Brazil did not have a national championship due to the sheer size of the country. Instead there were regional championships. Santos were in the Paulista, a strong championship with teams such as Sao Paolo and Corinthians. In 1958, Santos won the championship and were unstoppable, racking up scorelines such as 10-0, 9-1, 8-1 and 7-1. Pelé's record was astonishing, scoring a record 58 goals in 38 games.

The Rio and São Paolo teams rarely played each other in those days, which meant that Pelé did not match up against his international teammates on a regular basis. At the start of every year however, there was a tournament between the Rio and São Paolo teams. Santos won this championship in 1959, but lost the Paulista. Still, in the following three years, Santos won three consecutive Paulistas, and Pelé was top goal scorer in every one of them.

Santos had a number of exceptional footballers in those days. Midfielder Zito was a brilliant player, as was the winger Dorval. The legendary forward line of Pepe, Pagao, Coutinho and Pelé struck fear in all of their opponents. Coutinho and Pelé became known for 'tabelinhas' or one-twos, which always confused the opposition. Captain of the 1962 Brazil side, Mauro, was also in the team in defence, as was goalkeeper Gilmar, a vastly experienced Brazilian international. Santos were a formidable force in those years.

It was around this time that Pelé met Rosemeri, his first wife. Though Pelé was around three years her senior, the girl certainly caught Pelé's eye. They first met during a basketball match in which Rosemari was playing, but it was quite a while later before they met again. By chance, Pelé bumped into some of her basketball team mates and asked where Rosemeri worked. Once he found out, he made his way there to speak with her, and after some nervous conversation between the two, she told him to meet her one Saturday afternoon at her house. He met her parents that Saturday afternoon and everything ran very smoothly. Her parents were friendly and welcoming, and Pelé felt comfortable and at ease.

The Brazilian law at the time dictated that all male eighteen year-olds had to do a year of military service, and Pelé was no different. After his eighteenth birthday, Pelé was enlisted into the Sixth Group of the Motorised Coast Artillery in Santos. He was not given any special treatment for being a world champion, and worked just as anybody else would have done. He still played football during this time, for both club and country, as well as for his barracks' team who played against other barracks in Santos. It was a busy time for Pelé.

Pelé was sent off for the first time in his career when he was picked for the Army XI to play against an Argentinean side in the South American Military Championships. After being kicked and grabbed all game Pelé retaliated, and a fight broke out which led to Pelé being sent off.

After the World Cup win in 1958, Brazilian football became world famous, known for its skill, elegance and technique. Santos were seen as the finest proponents of the game domestically, and they were in high demand. The club went on tours regularly, usually to the Americas at the beginning of the year, and to Europe in the middle.

The schedule was as relentless as it was exhausting for Pelé. On nine occasions, Pelé played two matches within 24 hours, and on one occasion, he played three in 48 hours. He was playing for five teams: Santos, Brazil, an all-star São Paolo side, the barracks' team and the Army team. Nowadays, such a schedule would simply not occur. It is astounding that his legs were able to withstand the constant football.

On the first of many Santos trips abroad, the Brazilians played twenty-two games in just six weeks. They won thirteen, drew five and lost four, quite an achievement considering the games played and the distances travelled. One of the defeats came against the great Real Madrid side of the time, a team who had won every European cup there had been to date, and which included the exceptionally talented Alfredo di Stefano. The game was billed as the match to determine the best team in the world, but if truth be told, Santos were drained and lost 5-3.

In February 1961, Pelé picked up his first serious injury. Santos were playing Necaxa in Mexico City. The Santos players were exhausted and struggling to cope with the altitude. A collision with a Necaxa defender left Pelé with face and shoulder injuries, and, despite trying to get back up and play Pelé could not, and fainted soon after. He was injured for three weeks, though nothing was broken.

By March, Pelé was back at the top of his game. In a match at the Maracana against Fluminesne, Pelé scored what many consider to be his greatest goal. Pelé picked up the ball in his own penalty area and began dribbling, dancing around six players and then the goalkeeper, before hitting the ball home. It was a remarkable goal, and one which many Brazilians consider to be perfection. Disappointingly, there were no television cameras in the stadium that day to capture the goal. Only the people present in the stadium will have the pleasure of seeing that goal and having it imprinted in their memories forever.

Pelé still had problems with his shoulder and did not play for the whole European tour in 1961. He did return to the Santos side against Basel in Switzerland, and Santos won 8-2, Pelé scoring five of them. This prompted a pitch invasion from the Swiss to get up close to the magical Brazilians, which just goes to show the effect Brazilian football was having on football enthusiasts throughout the world.

Pelé was becoming unstoppable. In a three week period in September 1961, he scored twenty-three goals in six matches, quite an unbelievable feat. Santos were battering all teams before them, notching up ludicrous scorelines such as 8-0 and 10-1.

Pelé was becoming a national celebrity. Two books were released about his young life, and he was the subject of a biopic entitled *I Am Pelé*. European clubs were becoming very interested, and Internazionale offered to pay Pelé a huge amount of money to play for the Nerazzurri. Pelé refused, however, preferring to remain with Santos.

During one tour of Italy in 1961, the Juventus president, Umberto Agnelli, invited Pelé, the Santos president and a few others to lunch. Agnelli was courteous and polite and soon it became clear that he was interested in Santos' prized asset. The Santos president, shocked as he was, said that Pelé was not for sale. The Juventus president interrupted him and said, "So how about we start with one million dollars?" This was an absolutely exorbitant amount of money at the time, almost unthinkable. He also offered Pelé the equivalent of tens of millions of dollars in today's money to play for Juventus. This was money on a completely different scale. In spite of this, Pelé again rejected the offer. Whether Pelé could have actually moved abroad or not is debatable. The Brazilian Congress had actually realised the worth of Pelé to the country, and had labelled him as a "non-exportable national treasure".

Chapter 5: 1962 World Cup

For the 1962 World Cup in Chile, Brazil were favourites and the holders. The team consisted of much of the same players, including Zito, Vava, Didi, Garrincha, Gilmar, Zagallo and Pelé.

Pelé went into the tournament with a niggly groin strain, probably in large part due to the sheer amount of games Pelé had played over the past couple of years. Brazil was drawn against Mexico, Czechoslovakia and Spain. In the first game against Mexico, Brazil struggled, but their class eventually showed. Pelé assisted Zagallo for the first goal and then scored the second himself, a brilliant goal in which he took the ball past four defenders and drove a powerful shot past the Mexican goalkeeper.

In the second game, Brazil came up against a strong Czechoslovakian side. The game finished 0-0, but Pelé was in a mess. After starting the game well, he struck a shot towards goal, and immediately felt something pull in his groin. In those days, substitutes were not allowed, so Pelé could not be replaced. He played on in agony, but much to the credit of the Czechoslovakian side, they took it easy on Pelé, and did not kick him as they may have done if he had been fit. The Brazilian doctor confirmed that Pelé had gotten a severe muscle strain. Pelé would not play any further part in the World Cup of 1962.

Spain was Brazil's next opponent, and without Pelé, Brazil came out on top 2-1 to progress to the quarter-finals. Their next opponent was England, a team with top quality players such as Bobby Charlton, Jimmy Greaves and Bobby Moore. Garrincha was unstoppable in the quarter-final, scoring twice and dominating the game in a 3-1 victory for Brazil.

In the semi-final Brazil came up against host Chile. Garrincha was again outstanding, scoring twice and running rings around the Chileans, despite some awful tackles and treatment. The 1962 World Cup was Garrincha's World Cup without question. Pelé sat in the stands frustrated, still unable to play a part.

Pelé hoped he might make the final, but in the end, he was simply not fit enough, his groin causing him great pain. Pelé was inconsolable and wanted to take the plane back to Brazil immediately. However, after some persuasion, he remained in Chile, passing on his support to the team. Again, he watched from the stands, incredibly frustrated and disappointed. Brazil ended up winning 3-1 to claim their second World Cup triumph.

Pelé did not share the delight of his team mates, and was plagued with doubts about his future with the team and as a player. It was a time of mixed emotions and deep reflection for the twenty-one year-old. The values of dedication, honesty and humility which were instilled in him from a young age helped him. His family and friends helped drive him forward, and soon Pelé was back doing what he did best.

Chapter 6: Return to Form

Later in the year, Santos won the South American equivalent of the European Cup, the Libertadores Cup. This was the most prestigious club competition in the Western hemisphere. Pelé played in the playoff in Buenos Aires against the Uruguayan side Peñarol who had won the first two competitions. Pelé scored twice in a 3-0 victory to make Santos the champions. Santos also went on to win the Campeonato Brasiliero (A competition among all the state champions in Brazil) that same year, a competition in which Pelé scored 37 goals.

This victory meant that Santos would take on Benfica in the Intercontinental Club Cup, a match between the European Cup winners and Libertadores Cup winners. This was the Benfica side of the 'European Pelé' or the 'Black Panther', Eusebio, a player of extraordinary talent. The game was played over two legs, and the first-leg was played in the Maracana. Santos won 3-2 in a tight affair, Pelé scoring the first and third goals.

In the return leg, in Lisbon, Pelé played what he believes to be the best match of his career. Benfica were extremely confident of beating Santos, but much to their surprise, Santos stole the show. Pelé scored a hat-trick and set up one in a 5-2 victory. The second was a special goal, one where he dribbled past five players and hit a shot into the top right corner of the net. It was a mesmerising performance from Pelé, and even the Benfica crowd were applauding. It was a game in which Benfica simply could not cope with him. Santos played a game of footballing beauty. After the disappointment of Chile, this was a breath of fresh air for Pelé. It healed some of the wounds of the World Cup, and his questions and doubts were put to bed. 'The King' was back![7]

In 1963, Santos won the Taca Brasil for the third time in a row, which was essentially an early form of a proper Brazilian league, but was an altogether weaker competition than the Paulista.

[7] http://www.fifa.com/world-match-centre/news/newsid/178/290/3/index.html

In that same year, Santos won the Libertadores Cup for the second year in succession. In the semi-finals they met Rio team Botafogo, a team which included Garrincha and 1970 World Cup winner, Jairzinho. In the first leg, Pelé equalised in the last minute to earn Santos a 1-1 draw. In the return leg, Pelé's display was another master class in which he scored a hat-trick, and Santos won 4-0.

In the Libertadores Cup final of that year, Santos travelled to Buenos Aires to face Boca Juniors at the intimidating La Bonbonera stadium. In a manner typical of the treatment Pelé was dished out at the time, the Argentinians pushed and shoved him relentlessly, and even ripped his shorts. Despite this, Pelé scored the winner for Santos with only eight minutes left on the clock in a 2-1 victory.

In the Intercontinental Cup of 1963, Santos met AC Milan. They lost the first leg in Milan 4-2, with Pelé scoring both of Santos' goals. Pelé got injured and could not play in the return leg at the Maracana. In spite of Pelé's injury Santos won 4-2, setting up a playoff decider, which Santos won 1-0, meaning that Santos were South American and world champions again.

Santos was still a team of much admiration and fascination throughout football in 1963. The team was still engaged in tours around the world, and played over fifty matches abroad that year. Their European opponents would often engage in the more violent aspects of football, pulling of shirts, kicking, pushing and taunting. Pelé particularly was subjected to this type of conduct. It was the European way of containing the skillful football of the Brazilians, but it was as rough as it was unruly. Also, he would be a man marked throughout matches from the first whistle to the last. Opponents were doing everything in their power to stop Pelé, by any means possible, but in the main, they were unsuccessful.

In 1964, Santos did not retain the Libertadores Cup, but they did win the Paulista championship yet again, Pelé scoring 34 goals in the process, making him the top goal scorer in the competition for the eighth consecutive year (which would become nine the year after). They also won the Taca Brasil for the fourth consecutive year. On the 21st November 1964 Santos defeated Botafogo in the Paulista 11-0, and Pelé scored a remarkable eight goals in the victory.

In 1965 Santos put on a good showing in the Libertadores Cup and, as in 1962, they met Peñarol in the final. The game was tied after both legs, and so a play-off was played to decide the winner. Santos were defeated in the play-off 2-1. However, Santos did win the Paulista and Taca Brasil in 1965, and Pelé notched up 49 goals in the Paulista.

In 1965, Pelé was given the chance to exorcise some of the ghosts of 1962. Santos met a team consisting of a selection of Czechoslovak players in Chile. It is a game that went down in folklore, and has been dubbed as the best match that has ever taken place in Chile. Santos won 6-4, and Pelé scored a hat-trick, showing the Czechoslovak players just what he could do, having missed the World Cup final against them three years earlier.

A little earlier, in 1964, Santos had hired Professor Julio Mazzei as technical instructor, which was a real coup for the club. He was a cultured, educated man and he made a deep impression on Pelé. Indeed, Mazzei acted as a mentor for Pelé throughout his career. Pelé believes that either directly or indirectly, Mazzei influenced Pelé to finally tie the knot with Rosemeri. Despite the fact that Rosemeri was still cautious about marrying because of her young age, Pelé and his future mother-in-law believed that the time had come for marriage.

In 1966, Pelé and Rosemeri married. The ceremony was simple and unassuming, with just a few friends and the families of both Rosemeri and Pelé in attendance. The media swooped on the story and, to Pelé's anger, some articles were expressing their disapproval of a black man marrying a white woman. Race had never been a question in their relationship; they were just two people in love.

A few years earlier, Pelé had come into contact with a Spaniard known as Pepe Gordo. Pelé was keen to invest some of the money he was earning, and immediately took a liking to Gordo upon meeting him. He gave him power of attorney over his financial affairs and wanted Gordo to make a few good investments on Pelé's behalf. A few months before the wedding, it became clear that Pelé had some serious financial issues. Gordo admitted that the Pelé coffers were empty. The investments had turned disastrously, and in addition to this, Pelé owed a lot of money. Gordo had frittered away all of Pelé's money. Even if Pelé got rid of all of his assets, he would still owe money.

Pelé was naïve and had ignored the warning signs of Gordo's ineptness. Rosemeri had never trusted him, and Pelé's business partner and team mate Zito, had pulled out of dealings with Gordo a long time ago. Pelé felt foolish and stupid. Pelé did not want to claim for bankruptcy, so there was only one option. He had to borrow money to pay off his debts, and then work to restore his assets. Santos offered to put up the cash if Pelé signed a contract with very favourable terms to the club; Pelé had no choice but to accept.

Chapter 7: 1966 World Cup and Following Years

For the 1966 World Cup, Brazil was the clear favourite. Journalists, managers and supporters alike all thought it was inevitable; Brazil would win the World Cup for the third year in a row.

Brazil did not prepare in the same manner in which they had for the two previous tournaments. The Brazilian delegation was complacent and overly confident. The selection process itself was a shambles, with more than forty players making it into the initial World Cup squad. The squad was divided into four teams, and they were training in locations up and down Brazil. Even after the squad arrived in England the final selection was not known. There was animosity between the new head of the delegation, Carlos Nascimento, and the new coach, who had also coached the team during the 1958 World Cup win: Vicente Feola. The Brazilian Technical Commission as a whole was a farce, and there was an ill feeling throughout the Brazilian camp. There was no coherence to the preparation. It was confused, disorderly and ineffectual. All in all, it was terrible preparation, and the writing was on the wall for Brazil.

In Brazil's group were Bulgaria, Hungary and Portugal. Brazil's first match at the World Cup was against Bulgaria, and in a manner befitting of Brazil's woeful preparations for the World Cup, a team was fielded which had never started together before. Nonetheless, Brazil won 2-0 with two free kicks, one apiece from Pelé and Garrincha in each half. The Bulgarians were a physical team, and Pelé was getting kicked persistently from his marker.

Pelé was rested for Brazil's next game against Hungary due to his injury problems. In large part because of poor preparation, Pelé was not feeling fully fit, and Bulgaria's rough tactics certainly did not help his cause. If Brazil won, they would be through to the next round and a draw would have been a good result too. Brazil ended up losing 3-1. Hungary and Portugal were now both on four points each (in those days it was two points for a win). Unless Brazil won by a high score line against Portugal, the South Americans would be dumped out of the competition in the group stages.

It was a formidable task against a Portugal side which had many players from the great Benfica side of the time, including a striker in tremendous form, Pelé's old foe and friend, Eusebio. The Brazil selectors were in a panic and dropped a number of players including Garrincha and Djalma Santos. Pelé was not fully fit but was drafted back in, as was a player who had not played a World Cup match since 1958, Orlando.

Brazil ended up losing 3-1, Eusebio twice on the score sheet for Portugal. This was the match in which the famous pictures of Pelé being hacked down relentlessly were taken. The tackles from the Portuguese were simply atrocious. Shockingly, no player was sent off in spite of those horrendous challenges. Brazil was comprehensively beaten by Portugal and out of the World Cup. It was an extremely disappointing World Cup campaign for Brazil. Pelé stated that he would never play in a World Cup again following the dreadful Brazilian performance. He was dismayed by the aggressive tactics of opponents, disappointed with the abysmal officiating which allowed such tactics to go unpunished and with the woeful preparation of the Brazilian delegation.

1966 was not a year Pelé remembers with great fondness. He scored fewer goals than in any other season, and played fewer games too. One positive moment in this year for Pelé was Santos' victory in a competition in the USA in August. Internazionale and Benfica were two of the teams taking part in the tournament. When Santos met Benfica, it was almost like a repeat of the Brazil vs. Portugal match in England a couple of months earlier. Santos was desperate to show Benfica just what they could do. Santos ran out 4-0 winners with Pelé scoring the first. It was a great performance and one which enthralled the American crowd. In the final Santos met Internazionale and won 4-1. Santos had rekindled at least some of the greatness of Brazilian football.

In January of 1967, Rosemeri gave birth to her first child, a baby girl who was named Kelly Cristina. Despite this being a relatively hard time for Pelé, his first child gave him much happiness. He credits his new baby girl as helping him to rediscover his love for football.

In May of the same year, Santos made a trip to Africa. It was Pelé's first time in Africa, and the trip made a real impression on him and how he viewed the world. Santos toured Gabon, Congo, Senegal and the Ivory Coast. Hordes of fans watched Santos' games and followed them wherever they went. They particularly adored the King. Pelé felt that his success as a black man gave the people a sense of hope, a feeling of inspiration. Here was a man whose forefathers came from Africa and who was the greatest football player on the planet. It was a humbling experience for Pelé. He called it a fantastic education.

A match between Santos and an Olympic Columbian team in Bogota was a match which will forever remain in Pelé's memory. The referee, Guillermo "Chato" Velazquez let a goal stand against Santos which should have been disallowed. After furious arguments between the referee and Santos players, the referee decided to send off Santos player Lima, and then sent off Pelé, too. The Columbian crowd were furious and hysteric, many in attendance were there simply to see Pelé. They threw objects onto the pitch and were desperate to get at Chato, who was being protected by policemen with batons. The crowd started chanting "Pelé, Pelé, Pelé!" and in an unprecedented turn of events, Chato was sent off, and Pelé 'un sent-off!' Some of the Santos players were later arrested because of a complaint made by Chato! The Santos team missed their flight, and it was not until two days later that they finally boarded a plane to leave the Columbian capital. It was a fiasco, but certainly an eventful tour and probably one of Pelé's most memorable!

In early 1969 there was another Santos tour to Africa. This included a trip to Nigeria, a country in which a civil war was taking place. It is said that there was a 48 hour ceasefire between the Biafrans and Nigerian forces, just to allow Santos to play. Whether this is true or not is hard to ascertain, but Pelé recalls that there were white peace flags throughout the Nigerian capital Lagos when the Santos players arrived. Pelé's and Santos' global appeal and influence was evident.

Chapter 8: 1,000th Goal and 1970 World Cup

Towards the end of 1969, Pelé was closing in on an unbelievable record, the scoring of 1,000 goals in his career. Pelé edged nearer and nearer to the milestone, with the national and international press getting increasingly excited, travelling in huge numbers to every game Santos played. Pelé often scored more than one goal in a match, so it really could have been any match in which Pelé achieved the feat.

The feat was quite fittingly achieved in the Maracana stadium when Santos faced Vasco. It was the 19th November - Brazilian national flag day – and Pelé's beloved mother's birthday also. The stadium was filled to capacity. Vasco players were desperate to not allow themselves to be the opponents which Pelé scored his 1,000th goal against. Much to their dismay, Pelé was tripped in the penalty box as he made a run into the box, and a penalty was given. The time had come. Up stepped Pelé, with the chance to score his 1,000th career goal. Pelé remembers, "For the first time in my career I felt nervous. I had never felt a responsibility like this before. I was shaking".

Pelé was not actually a regular penalty taker, but he had taken a penalty or two in the last few games. Pelé's way of taking penalties was influenced by a penalty he saw taken by Didi back in 1959. It involved running towards the ball, stopping just before hitting the ball, looking to see where the goalkeeper was positioned, and then striking the ball in the direction which the goalkeeper was furthest away from. In Brazil it is known as the 'Paradinha'.

Pelé executed a Parandinha, and scored. He had done it. 1,000 career goals for Pelé! The stadium erupted with firecrackers and cheers and Pelé grabbed the ball from the net and kissed it. The pressure Pelé felt to reach 1,000 goals was finally lifted. Play was stopped for 20 minutes as Pelé was surrounded by journalists and photographers. He dedicated the goal to the children of Brazil. He was hoisted on the shoulders of somebody and did a lap around the pitch, overcome with emotion and crying profusely.

Pelé was called to the national team in early 1969 and had originally refused to play. However, considering his current form, and with the prospect of representing Brazil again at the World Cup, Pelé had a change of heart. He would play for Brazil in the World Cup for the fourth time. Pelé was also determined not to go out as a loser with Brazil, considering the team's performance at the 1966 World Cup. Pelé felt he had something to prove.

Brazil's preparation for the 1970 World Cup in Mexico was far superior to that of 1966. There were changes in the administration of the team. The general atmosphere in the Brazil camp was far more relaxed and there was none of the complacency of 1966. The preparation was very professional and sophisticated. Pelé's old Brazil team mate Mario Zagallo was the coach for Brazil, and he hired some technical staff for the tournament. There was even detailed analysis of every player's physiology.

Pelé felt an affinity with the Mexican crowds and stadiums after Santos' many visits there, and the spectators had always treated them well. Brazil's qualification for the tournament was simple enough with six victories in as many matches. Pelé scored six goals, and the team was playing in perfect harmony. It was perfect preparation for the tournament.

Many in the press were complaining about playing Pelé and Tostao in the same team due to their similar positions, and there were also complaints of a similar nature about playing Gerson and Rivelino in the same team. Despite the criticisms, coach Zagallo maintained that he would play the best, most intelligent players, and that was final.

Pelé deems that a central factor in the success of Brazil's 1970 World Cup campaign was prayer, believing that it united them as a team. After a phone conversation with Rosemeri, he learnt that all his family were praying for them. He thought it would be fantastic to incorporate praying into the Brazil camp. The players would pray almost every day throughout the tournament. Initially, just Pelé, Rogerio and Carlos Alberto prayed, but by the end of the tournament almost all the Brazil camp were praying in tandem. They didn't pray to win the World Cup as one might expect. They prayed for a multitude of other things such as the war in Vietnam, or for the health of somebody who needed it.

Brazil's first game was against Czechoslovakia on 3 June 1970. Some of the press prior to the tournament had been writing Brazil off, claiming that it was a team with attack but no defence, and that Pelé was a spent force. Foolish words indeed! The team lined up as follows: Felix, Carlos Alberto, Brito, Piazza, Everaldo, Clodoaldo, Gerson, Jairzinho, Tostao, Rivelino, Pelé. It was a magical team, filled with exceptionally gifted players.

Such critics would have felt some justification in their criticisms when Czechoslovakia took the lead. Rivelino equalised just ten minutes later though, with a powerfully struck free-kick. Soon after that kick came a moment of World Cup folklore. Pelé picked up the ball from Clodoaldo just before the half-way line in the centre circle, and spotted the Czechoslovakian goalkeeper off his line. In a moment of ingenuity, audacity and brilliance, Pelé struck a powerful shot from inside his own half, catching the goalkeeper completely off guard. The ball flew towards goal, looping over the goalkeeper's head, and as he scrambled back in desperation, the ball slid just inches wide. It was so nearly the most extraordinary of goals. Nevertheless, it was a moment that will never be forgotten in footballing circles.

In the second-half, Pelé did score. He met a high cross from Gerson on his chest beautifully, before casually striking a half-volley into the far corner, giving the goalkeeper absolutely no chance, making it 2-1. It was a sublime piece of control by Pelé. The goal scoring winger Jairzinho added two more, and the score ended up 4-1 to Brazil.

Brazil's next opponents were the holders, England. The team still boasted some brilliant players such as Bobby Charlton, Bobby Moore and Gordon Banks. This was the match everybody had been waiting for.

In the opening stages of the match, another moment in this World Cup which will never be forgotten took place, and again it involved Pelé. Jairzinho skipped past his marker and delivered a cross towards the far post. Pelé, with a jump in the air to rival any high jumper, met the cross superbly, and powered a header downwards toward the goal; the outcome seemed a certainty. But suddenly, Gordon Banks appeared out of nowhere and made what many believe to be the greatest save of all time. He raced across his goal line, and as Pelé's header bounced upwards towards the back of the net, Banks threw himself to his right and tipped the ball over the crossbar with his arm, making the most incredible of saves. Pelé was shocked. The crowd were shocked. England's defence were shocked. It was a memorable moment.

It was a tight affair, but eventually England caved in. After some great work by Tostao, the ball was chipped to Pelé just inside the area and he calmly played a ball to his right which Jairzinho met and fired into the top corner, to give Brazil a hard-fought 1-0 victory.

Brazil's final match in the group stages came against Romania. Brazil was not at their best, and even seemed a little complacent. Still, they won 3-2 with two goals from Pelé and one from Jairzinho.

In the quarter-finals, Brazil met Peru in an all-South American affair. Peru were managed by Pelé's old teammate, Didi. It was a typically attacking match between the two South-American sides, and Pelé remembers the match fondly. It finished 4-2, with goals from Rivelino, two from Tostao and one from Jairzinho. The semi-finals awaited Brazil.

Brazil would face Uruguay in the semi-finals. Thoughts of the 1950 World Cup and all the dismay that followed it consumed Pelé's thoughts. Brazil had not faced Uruguay in the World Cup since that day. It was a match which the whole team was desperate to win. To be victorious would be to get the monkey off their backs.

There were a lot of nerves in the Brazilian camp before the match, and it was difficult to remain calm. Brazil began the game in much the same way as Brazil had in 1950; bad passes, weak defending and the inability to get through their opponents.

After twenty minutes, Uruguay struck to make it 1-0. The Uruguayans were keen to upset the Brazilians just like in 1950, and played defensively, aggressively and intensely. Pelé was on the receiving end of many bad tackles, and at one point Pelé retaliated by elbowing an opponent in the forehead. It was a physical and rough affair.

Just before half-time, Clodoaldo equalised for Brazil and the sides went in level at the break. In the second-half, Brazil put on the gas and began to control the game with some brilliant attacking play. Jairzinho and Rivelino both scored, and Brazil were 3-1 up. During the second-half, yet another unforgettable World Cup moment took place, and yet again it involved Pelé. A through-ball was played to him, and as he saw the goalkeeper racing off his line he opted to dummy the goalkeeper instead of meeting the pass, allowing the ball to continue its course to the right. He bamboozled the goalkeeper by running to the goalkeeper's left, and as the ball trickled on in the other direction, he arced his run back towards the ball and hit a shot goalwards, which agonisingly trickled past the post of the empty net. It was so nearly yet another unbelievable goal from the twenty-nine year old. The match finished 3-1.

Brazil met Italy in the final who had beaten Franz Beckenbauer's West Germany in the semi-final 4-3. It was a sweltering June afternoon in the Azteca Stadium, and the audience watching the match worldwide was believed to be nearly 1 billion people, with 100,000 spectators in the stadium. Brazil's line-up was the same as the first match and the semi-final. It was to be the attacking brilliance of Brazil against the sturdy defence of Italy. Italy's team included the great Italian full-back Giacinto Facchetti as well as forwards Angelo Domenghini and Luigi Riva. It was a match not to be forgotten, as Brazil put on a master class.

Pelé scored Brazil's first goal with a sumptuous header. Rivelino delivered a high cross into the box, and again Pelé's leap into the air was quite incredible. He connected with the ball high in the air, towering above his marker, and arrowed a header into the bottom corner of the net; a brilliant goal. Italy equalised not too long before half-time, and at the interval it was 1-1. Italy was not offering much in attack, defending deeply and seemingly content with their counter-attacking method.

After sixty-six minutes, Brazil was back ahead after Gerson hit a powerful long-range effort into the bottom corner. 2-1 to Brazil and all the momentum was with the South Americans. Jairzinho scrambled in a third, and in the process, he became the only player in World Cup history to score in every match in every round of the competition.

The final goal in the match will always be remembered as one of the very finest the world has ever seen. It was a goal befitting of a team of such astonishing talent, a team which many consider to be the greatest of all time. After a couple of passes between the Brazilians, Clodoaldo picked up the ball and skipped past four challenges with incredible skill and ease, before passing to Rivelino. Rivelino then played a ball upfield to Jairzinho on the left wing. Jairzinho went inwards, and played a neat pass to Pelé. Pelé showing such control and class masterfully took the ball under close control, taking a couple of touches with either foot, patiently waiting for the run of Carlos Alberto. Pelé then nonchalantly laid the ball to his right, into the space which Carlos Alberto was steaming towards. Carlos Alberto met the pass like a bulldozing train, and smashed the ball into the far corner of the Italian goal. It was a beautiful goal, and a goal which epitomised this quite spectacular football team.

There was pandemonium when the final whistle went. Brazil's players were mobbed by reporters and spectators and it would be several minutes before they could make their way to the changing rooms. Once in there, Pelé gave his thanks to God and his family for the victory. When the team returned to the pitch they collected the trophy and there were many tears of joy. Pelé, now a World Cup winner for the third time, appreciated with more clarity and maturity just how special it was to win this trophy. He understood just what it would mean to everybody in Brazil. Brazil was comprehensively world champions for the third time and would keep the Jules Rimet trophy.

Chapter 9: Post-World Cup

Pelé quickly left the Brazilian celebrations, when he finally got the chance to speak to Rosemeri. She told him that she wanted Pelé by her side for her second pregnancy. She gave birth on 27th August 1970 to a baby boy named Edson Cholbi do Nascimento, or Edinho.

Pelé was now a mature adult, and it was around this time that thoughts of quitting football floated around his head. He was keen to get a proper education, and realised just how useful this would be in his later life. He acknowledged that he was not exactly an educated man. Becoming properly educated would also be a great example for his children. Pelé, with the help of mentor Julio Mazzei, began to study Physical Education, and it was Pelé's goal to study the subject at university. He studied in his spare time for a couple of years, and eventually he passed a set of exams which enabled him to enrol at the University of Santos for a three year degree in Physical Education. A few years later, Pelé graduated. He did not complete this degree as a stepping stone to coaching football as one might expect. It was simply something he did to increase his education and to set a good example to his children.

Pelé now indicated his long term intentions to both Santos and Brazil. He did not intend to carry on playing for many more years, and he was determined to retire whilst still playing his football at a high level. Pelé now had two children and he was concerned about the burden being placed on Rosemeri.

Pelé played his final two matches for Brazil within the space of a week. The first was on 11 July 1971 against Austria in São Paolo. Pelé played for just the first half, but managed a goal, taking him to 77 goals for Seleção, which is still a Brazil record. The final match was fittingly at the Maracana, on 18th July 1971, against Yugoslavia. There were 180,000 in the crowd to witness Pelé's last match for Brazil. Pelé was a little overwhelmed by the whole occasion, and again only played the first half. At the end of the match, he made a lap of the stadium and the crowd cried "Fica! Fica!" ("Stay! Stay!") Pelé was in a flood of tears, but his mind was already made up.

Pelé's time at Santos was also beginning to come to a close. Despite three consecutive Paulista championship victories in 1967, '68 and '69, the club had essentially been in decline since around 1966, and Pelé was becoming more insignificant in the club's limited successes.

Santos were making a huge number of trips abroad during the late 1960s and early 1970s, including to the Caribbean, North America, Europe, Asia, Australia and around South America. It was an extremely hectic schedule, and was beginning to take its toll on Pelé. Towards the end of his time for the club, Pelé was not really enjoying his football. There were also changes to the management of the club at many levels, and Pelé was becoming more and more disillusioned. There were also rumours being circulated that Pelé was demanding more money from the club, and as a result, he was getting richer at the expense of the club, who was getting poorer. Pelé maintains that this was not the case.

Pelé wanted to play for a year on his own terms, and then play for a year on a basic salary, with prize money and fees during that year going directly to charity. Pelé's offer was eventually accepted by Santos. Santos continued on their tours, but it was not the same as the golden years. Santos was a shadow of the team they were. During one tour in England, they lost 2-1 to Fulham and 3-2 to Plymouth which goes to show just how much the team had declined.

There was one noteworthy moment for Pelé in June of 1973. In a game in the United States, Santos played the Baltimore Bays, and Pelé scored a goal directly from a corner.

In fact, Pelé's links to America were becoming more and more entrenched. He had met the head of the New York Cosmos in 1971, and the idea of playing in America did appeal to Pelé, if not immediately. Furthermore, in 1973, Pelé signed a contract with American company Pepsi-Cola to work on a worldwide project of football workshops for children. Pelé travelled with Julio Mazzei to sixty-four countries, giving workshops throughout the world.

Santos did manage some success in 1973 when they were crowned joint champions of the Paulista championship. Pelé was top goal scorer in the competition. All in all, during Pelé's career with Santos he was top goal scorer on eleven occasions, and Santos won the Paulista ten times.

Pelé's time at Santos was coming to an end. Despite his good form and goals, he did not have the same attachment with the club he did during the golden years. He made Santos aware that his final match would be at the end of September against Ponte Preta.

During the match, in typical Pelé fashion, he did something completely spontaneous, but not what one might expect. With about twenty minutes played, a pass was lofted over to him, and instead of controlling it, he caught the ball, much to the shock of the players and the crowd. He then jogged to the centre spot, placed the ball down, and knelt down before it, before lifting his arms out like an aeroplane's wings. He wanted to thank all the people there, the Santos supporters, all Brazilians and God. Tears were streaming down his face as he turned slowly and faced all corners of the ground, saluting the fans. The crowd rose and roared in approval and respect. He then ran towards the Santos supporters, thanking them for all their support after eighteen years of football for the club. Pelé's Santos career was over, and what a career it had been!

Chapter 10: Financial Problems and New York Cosmos

Pelé encountered some more problems financially during this period in his life. His business venture with the parts manufacturer, Fiolax, was proving to be disastrous as the company started losing lots of money. Pelé had quite foolishly signed a note which had guaranteed a bank loan for the company and liabilities, regardless of the fact that he was not a majority shareholder. Pelé's losses in the end equated to a couple of million dollars. Once again, Pelé's finances were in a dreadful state.

With the help of João Havelange, the man who Pelé helped during his FIFA presidency bid in 1974, Pelé managed to not get into any *really* serious financial problems. Still, Pelé realised that he was going to have to start making some money again. Moreover, he did not want Fiolax to go bankrupt. Pelé decided he may need to return to the game. There were offers from the likes of Juventus and Real Madrid, but Pelé was adamant that he would not return to a life of football similar to that he lived whilst playing for Santos, and so refused their 15 million dollar offers.

But there was still one very interesting offer on the table, the New York Cosmos offer. Pelé discussed the possibilities of the move with Mazzei. Pelé was concerned about how the news would be received in Brazil and was cautious. He was already being criticised for retiring so early from both the national team and Santos. He was also worried about the impact the move would have on his family. Mazzei discussed with Pelé how the game was still in its infancy in the United States, and how Pelé could help promote the game there.

Pelé was eventually convinced by Mazzei's words. It was an exciting new adventure for Pelé, and an opportunity which he thought was too good to pass up. The contract which was eventually signed after months of deliberations was the biggest sport contract that had ever been signed at the time. The New York Cosmos had just signed the biggest name in football! Pelé was not signed purely for his footballing talents; there was a huge amount of money to be made by marketing the global name of Pelé. Mazzei was hired as assistant coach for the New York Cosmos. Pelé's and Mazzei's families made the trip to the Big Apple soon after.

On the 11th June 1975 Cosmos were ready to unveil their new star signing. They did so at the glamorous 21 Club and there was an enormous media presence, all keen to see the new kid on the block. Pelé's first match for the club was a week later against the Toronto Metros, which they won 2-0. The attendance shot up from 8,000 to 22,500 (more than capacity), which was an indication of the interest Pelé had garnered already amongst the American public. That season was a difficult one for the Cosmos and they won just six of their remaining fixtures, whilst losing seven. The Cosmos were simply not very good, and their fitness levels were not at the levels of other clubs in the league.

Some signings were made and Cosmos went on a couple of tours, including to Europe and the Caribbean. They also signed a couple of other South American players, and they were now becoming a much better team, to the delight of Pelé who had been concerned about the lack of quality in the side.

Pelé's family were taking well to New York, and soon they had a permanent apartment on the east side of Manhattan. The children were adapting to the new country and culture well, especially Edinho. Pelé was also beginning to become more and more famous, getting recognised in the States just as any baseball or American football player would.

It was around this time that Pelé coined his famous phrase of football being 'the beautiful game'. During interviews with American broadcasters, he would often be asked about soccer, to which he replied that the game he played was football to him and the rest of the world. He made a distinction between American football and football/soccer by labelling football as he knew it as "the beautiful game". One can only wonder what American audiences thought of this statement!

This period of time in New York was an exciting one. It was the age of parties and big disco nightclubs. Pelé, being the celebrity he was, met all sorts of musicians, actors and celebrities. The owners of New York Cosmos, Warner Communications, also owned music and film businesses, and consequently Warner parties were often ones filled with celebrities and stars. Pelé was becoming such a household name that even the likes of Robert Redford were getting ignored in favour of the Brazilian!

Pelé is known as being a teetotaller, but this is not exactly true, and it was during his time at the Cosmos that he began to drink (though to this day he only drinks on special occasions). In March, at the start of the season, it was still bitterly cold in New York, and many of the Latin players were struggling with the temperatures. As a way of warming them up, the team doctor allowed the Latin players to have a dram of whiskey before training!

New York Cosmos changed managers for the new season, and signed some more players from abroad, but the results remained patchy. The new manager, former Everton player Ken Furphy, favoured a more cautious approach than his predecessor, and Pelé was actually moved to midfield. Eventually, Furphy was replaced by the previous coach, Gordon Bradley, and results began picking up. Cosmos ended up finishing second in the Northern Division, and after a victory against Washington in the play-offs, Cosmos faced the Tampa Bay Rowdies in the final. The Cosmos ended up losing 3-1 to a superior side, but it was a gallant effort from the Cosmos.

At the end of the 1976 season, Pelé reached the landmark of 1,250 career goals, and was presented with a gold-encrusted boot at the 21 Club. It was another remarkable achievement.

Pelé signed a one year contract extension to play on until the end of 1977. The Cosmos signed the German legend Franz Beckenbauer as well as Carlos Alberto in July of that year. Attendance in American stadiums was growing, and the American media were becoming increasingly interested in the game. Pelé had certainly made an impact on the popularity of the game up and down the country.

Cosmos were playing brilliantly in 1977, winning their last eight home games to finish second in their division. The Cosmos defeated their conquerors of the previous season, the Tampa Bay Rowdies 3-0 on their way to winning the North American Soccer League Championship. They faced the Seattle Sounders in Portland, Oregon on the 27th August for the NASL Championship. The Cosmos won 2-1 to become NASL champions. This turned out to be Pelé's last competitive match. Pelé had scored an impressive 65 goals in 111 matches for the Cosmos. There were a couple of trips abroad after the match, before Pelé played in his final match against his beloved Santos. Pelé would play a half for both sides.

It was 1st October 1977 and 75,000 people were in attendance for Pelé's farewell match at the Giants Stadium in New Jersey. After twenty-one years of treating football fans worldwide to his special way of playing the game, Pelé's incredible football career would soon be at an end. The match finished 2-1 to the Cosmos, with Pelé scoring one of Cosmos' goals. At the final whistle Pelé felt just as much emotion as he had after his previous two farewell matches, for Brazil and Santos. Tears were streaming down his face, with Pelé utterly overwhelmed. The players carried Pelé around the pitch as the rain poured down, and there was sadness in everybody's eyes in the realisation that this unique footballer would never grace a football pitch again.

Amongst all the commotion, Pelé spotted his father and Waldemar de Brito standing under an umbrella, and suddenly a vivid recollection came over Pelé as he remembered the journey the three took over twenty years ago to Santos. If not for Waldemar's persuasions all those years ago, things could have been so very different, not just for Pelé and his family, but for football in general.

The career of the biggest name in football was over and as he made his way around the pitch, thoughts of his mother and God pervaded in his head. There was a huge party later at the Plaza. In attendance were many of Pelé's friends and family, including his parents, the World Cup-winning Brazil captains Bellini, Mauro and Carlos Alberto, Bobby Moore and Franz Beckenbauer and Boxing legend Muhammed Ali. Pelé did go on to play a few tribute games, but his career was over. Pelé's final stats were as follows: 1,367 games played, 1,283 goals scored; quite astonishing.

Pelé again retired as a champion, and felt as if his mission to increase the appeal and scope of football in the States had been achieved.

Chapter 11: Post-Football Days

On the 27th September 1978, Pelé was made a 'citizen of the world' by the United Nations, something which Pelé holds very dearly. In his retirement, Pelé also became more involved with FIFA, encouraging higher standards of refereeing and stronger punishments for players who deliberately went out to hurt players. Rough tackling and poor refereeing were two of Pelé's pet peeves during his playing days, and he was determined to take action on these issues. Pelé also became a Goodwill Ambassador for UNICEF, and took on a role of an ambassadorial nature for FIFA.

In 1978, Rosemeri gave birth to her third child, Jennifer. Pelé at the time was commentating on the 1978 World Cup in Argentina, and missed the birth. Rosemeri was not impressed to say the least. She was also not happy with all his engagements and his constant travelling abroad either. Rosemeri wanted a divorce, which happened not long after.

Furthermore, it became clear that Pelé had not been behaving faithfully with Rosemeri. He had a couple of flings whilst he was with Rosemeri, one whilst they were married, and one whilst they were dating. He fathered two girls with these two women.

After the divorce, Pelé decided to stay in New York and signed a ten-year contract with Warner, doing promotional work for the company. Pelé started behaving quite promiscuously during this period of his life, having a whole host of flings with quite a number of different women. He also attended many parties and actually became a good friend of another footballer more than partial to a party or two, George Best.

Pelé married for a second time in 1994 to Assiria Seixas Lemos. The pair had met some years earlier, but it was not until the early 1990s that they began to date. The pair moved to Brazil after marrying, and two years later, Assiria gave birth to twins, Joshua and Celeste (the girl named after Pelé's mother). Pelé and Assiria are still together to this day.

In 1990, Pelé ventured out into the sports business. He established 'Pelé Sports & Marketing'. The idea was to manage Pelé's profile and further the interests of football in Brazil. The company also invested in tournaments and television rights. Pelé eventually closed down the company when he became aware of maladministration within the company.

Pelé had spent much of his time in FIFA pushing for a World Cup to be hosted in America. Eventually this came about in 1994, but this was after Pelé had far fewer ties with the organisation, having fallen out with João Havelange. There was a big public row between Pelé and the Brazilian Football Confederation (CBF) about TV rights in 1994. Havelange took the side of the CBF president, Ricardo Teixeira, and, much to Pelé's dismay, he was not invited to the 1994 World Cup draw.

Surprisingly, Pelé was never really interested in professional football coaching. Yet Pelé did become attracted to the managerial side of things, and took a position with the Santos board. It was during a disorganised and fraught time for the club. Pelé did not enjoy the experience and decided he would not take such a position again.

In 1995, Pelé took a position in government as Minister for Sport. This made Pelé the first black man to be made a government minister in Brazil. Pelé, Assiria and his children relocated to the Brazilian capital, Brasilia. Pelé wanted to first transform Brazilian clubs into proper businesses, run in a professional and ethical way, and to make footballers "free agents" so that they were free to consider their options at the end of a contract with a club (what in Europe was known as the Bosman ruling). This did not go down well amidst all the corruption of Brazilian politics and sport.

Pelé was making more enemies than friends. It was a difficult time for Pelé and he struggled to push any kind of legislation through government. His ministry was even accused of corruption itself. One thing he did achieve was the initiation of a programme to build sports centres throughout Brazil, helping to keep youngsters out of a life of crime and trouble. In 1998, Pelé's work towards implementing a Brazilian version of the Bosman ruling bore some fruit when a law was enacted which freed the shackles Brazilian players had traditionally felt at the end of their contracts with their clubs.

The darkest days of Pelé's life came when his son, Edinho, was arrested for drug trafficking in 2005 (Edinho had also been arrested for a year and a half in 1992 after indirectly being involved in an illegal street race in which a person was killed). Pelé had spent years campaigning against the abuse of drugs and alcohol – and still does to this day; it all seemed a little ironic. Pelé was filled with guilt, rage and anger, all the negative emotions which were the complete opposite of his happiest playing days. It was the toughest time of Pelé's life. At the end of 2005, an order was given which gave Edinho liberty during his trial, allowing Edinho to be kept out of prison, but in February 2006, Edinho was again arrested. Edinho has since been sentenced to 33 years in jail for drug trafficking in May 2014.

Pelé likes to make a distinction between Edson and Pelé, highlighting a difference between the footballer and the man. He describes Edson as the person who is calm, relaxed, enjoys the countryside and fishing, spending time with his family, the more simple things in life. Pelé, in contrast, is the huge worldwide name, the man who transcends continents, the man who everybody knows. Pelé is ultimately an international brand. For over half a century Pelé has put his name to many products and has appeared in countless articles, programmes, documentaries, books, films, advertisements and more.

Pelé has several homes, and generally spends the summer months in New York, which for Pelé is like a second home. When the winter months arrive in the northern hemisphere, he spends his time in São Paolo, and in Guaruja, on the coast near Santos. He still lives with Assiria and their two children, who both go to school in São Paolo.

Pelé has one place where he feels most at ease and relaxed. It is a ranch in the state of São Paolo, about one hundred miles southwest of the capital, surrounded by nature. It is here where Pelé can forget about the obligations he has in being one of the most famous sportsmen in the world.

Pelé's main focus these days is his work with children. His continuous work with children, on a global scale, is a permanent fixture in his life, and that is the way he likes it.

Pelé is still involved with FIFA in one capacity or another, and is a worldwide ambassador for football. In August of 2010, Pelé was named as an Honorary President of New York Cosmos.

In February of 2012, 'Legends 10' was given exclusive rights to represent the brand of Pelé worldwide, bringing all managing and marketing of the brand under one agency, operating from New York and Los Angeles.

Also in 2012, Pelé was awarded with an honorary degree from the University of Edinburgh celebrating his contribution to humanitarian and environmental causes.

He has caused some controversy in recent years for his conservative views and remarks in general. He has also been criticised for his lack of sympathy with the concerns of average Brazilians. Many have been demonstrating for the last couple of years against corruption and poor living standards and wages. He was quoted as saying that Brazilians "should forget the demonstrations" and support the national team.

He is not universally loved in Brazil, and there are many who do take a dislike to him. He has been involved in disputes and arguments with many people in media, politics and sport, including ex Brazilian footballers such as Ronaldo and Romario. Nevertheless, Pelé is an absolutely huge, global name who is adored by masses of people both in Brazil and throughout the world. He is an iconic figure.

Chapter 12: Legacy

The legacy of Pelé will live on forever. The way he played the game was unprecedented. Along with his Santos and Brazil teammates, he transformed the way football was played and thought of; the Brazilians were teachers to the world of how to play the beautiful game. Pelé played football during a more innocent time, particularly in his earlier years, a time in which players cared more about scoring goals than their next pay check. The bottom line is that he was a man who simply loved to play the game.

He was in many ways the complete footballer. He was an athlete in being quick, agile and alert, whilst also possessing incredible technique, skill and intelligence on the pitch. He was two-footed, he could head the ball superbly, he could dribble past players with ease, he could score goals from any angle, he was a goal poacher, he was even the reserve goalkeeper for Brazil and Santos! He was a phenomenon.

Pelé's stats are quite incredible. In 1,367 games (including friendlies and tour matches), he scored 1,281 goals; in 92 official games for Brazil, he scored 77 goals; he scored 92 hat-tricks, scored four goals on 31 occasions, five on six occasions, and once scored eight. He won three World Cups (the only player to do so); two Intercontinental Cups and ten Paulista championships. He was top goalscorer in eleven Paulista championships and is the youngest ever goalscorer in a World Cup final. He was voted as the greatest ever footballer by former Ballon D'Or winners in *France Football* magazine and was voted as 'World Player of the Century' by the International Federation of Football History and Statistics. He was also voted as the 'Athlete of the Century' by the International Olympic Committee.[8] These are just a tiny handful of the achievements of Pelé. The list would simply be far too big to document all of his achievements.

---

[8] http://www.fifa.com/world-match-centre/news/newsid/132/191/7/index.html.

Many do consider Pelé to be the greatest footballer of all time. He was the first global football superstar. His popularity transcends countries and continents, and to this day he is still adored by hordes of people of all ages, from all corners of the globe. Wherever Pelé graced football pitches, whether it was in Asia, the Americas, Europe or anywhere else, a contagious sense of excitement filled the air. This was a player people paid to see.

Many greats of the game have lauded praise onto Pelé. "Pelé was the only footballer who surpassed the boundaries of logic", Johan Cruyff; "The greatest player in history was Di Stefano. I refuse to classify Pelé as a player. He was above that", Ferenc Puskas; "I told myself before the game, 'he's made of skin and bones just like everyone else'. But I was wrong", Tarcisio Burgnic *(THE ITALY DEFENDER WHO MARKED PELÉ IN THE MEXICO 1970 FINAL).* "When I saw Pelé play, it made me feel I should hang up my boots", Just Fontaine.[9] This debate about the player of the century is absurd. There's only one possible answer: Pelé. He's the greatest player of all time, and by some distance I might add", Zico.[10]

---

[9]

http://www.fifa.com/classicfootball/players/player=63869/quotes.html.

"Pelé was the most complete player I've ever seen, he had everything. Two good feet. Magic in the air. Quick. Powerful. Could beat people with skill. Could outrun people. Only 5 ft 8 in tall, yet he seemed a giant of an athlete on the pitch. Perfect balance and impossible vision. He was the greatest because he could do anything and everything on a football pitch", Bobby Moore.[11] "The best player ever? Pelé. Lionel Messi and Cristiano Ronaldo are both great players with specific qualities, but Pelé was better", Alfredo di Stefano.[i] There are many more players, managers and football experts who have similar sentiments.

It can never be said in certainty that Pelé is the greatest footballer of all time, but looking at his stats, achievements, and plaudits from all angles, it is hard to argue against it. It is impossible to think of the history of football, and not think of Pelé, and, moreover, to consider the possibility of Pelé having never adorned a professional football pitch. Pelé was a master, the King, a simply phenomenal footballer whose like we will probably never see again.

---

[10] http://www.independent.co.uk/sport/football/worldcup/pele-the-perfect-player-743002.html.

[11] http://www.espnfc.com/story/1155287.

47153710R00053

Made in the USA
San Bernardino, CA
23 March 2017